ENDORSEMENTS

"I have known Nancy Alcorn for many years and have always admired her compassion for and dedication to young women in need. The *Mercy for . . .* series examines real problems faced by young women today and provides the answers they need to move from a life of hurt and disappointment to one of hope and freedom."

—Victoria Osteen
Co-pastor, Lakewood Church

"I know all too well how the world places an overemphasis on what we see on the outside, and girls often resort to self-destructive patterns. I personally support the work of Mercy Ministries because I have seen first hand the changed lives."

—Niki Taylor
International Supermodel

"Mercy Ministries is not afraid to deal with the ugly, tough stuff—sexual abuse, cutting, addictions, eating disorders. Nancy and her Mercy Ministries team get to the core issues. If you have a daughter, work with girls, or are a young woman struggling with these issues . . . you want to hear what Nancy has to say. It is sure to change your life."

—CeCe Winans
Grammy Award-Winning Recording Artist

"I have personally known young women who have found healing through the principles in these books. This series is very timely in an age where little hope is given for young women struggling with these issues. Nancy Alcorn is not afraid to tell the truth and offer real hope through forgiveness and restoration. If you are desperate for hope or affected by a hopeless life, read through this series and find real answers."

—Sue Semrau
Head Women's Basketball Coach, Florida State University

"As a father of two girls in their late teens, I certainly know what girls face today. I have watched Nancy Alcorn and Mercy Ministries bring hope and healing to struggling young women for many years—young women who are completely without hope. The *Mercy for* . . . series reveals the Mercy Ministries difference and offers great inspiration, hope, and a way to true healing for all who want to be free."

—Dave Ramsey
Financial Expert and Author of *The Total Money Makeover*

TRAPPED

THE **MERCY FOR** SERIES

TRAPPED

Mercy for Addictions

NANCY ALCORN

WINEPRESS **WP** PUBLISHING

WinePress Publishing (PO Box 428, Enumclaw, WA 98022) functions only as book publisher. As such, the ultimate design, content, editorial accuracy, and views expressed or implied in this work are those of the author.

This book contains advice and information relating to mental and physical health. It is not intended to replace medical advice and should be used to supplement rather than replace regular care by your physician or mental health care professional. Readers are encouraged to consult their physicians or mental health care professionals with specific questions and concerns.

ISBN 13: 978-1-57921-934-5
ISBN 10: 1-57921-934-9
Library of Congress Catalog Card Number: 2007937885

DEDICATION

To those who are **desperate** for help
but feel there is no hope.
This book has been placed in your **hands** for a reason—
it is no accident that you are reading this even now.
My **prayer** is that you will read on,
because this book was written for you.
If you receive its message,
you will **never** be the same!
—*Nancy Alcorn*

CONTENTS

ACKNOWLEDGMENTS

I would like to thank the Mercy Ministries' staff members who have spent countless hours working on this manuscript with a heart to help people—Sherry Douglas, Sharon Manuel, Cissy Etheridge, Cassidy Carlgren, Amanda Phillips, and Ima Dixon.

Thanks to the Mercy residents who read the manuscript and provided honest feedback, helping to ensure the most meaningful and relevant material.

I offer a heartfelt thanks to our friends and supporters throughout the world who give so generously to bring forth changed lives.

Last but not least, I have such gratitude for our faithful staff in the various homes around the world. They give so much every day, and their love and compassion is evident. Thank you for serving alongside me in this global vision. You guys amaze me!

One hundred percent of all royalties and profits from this book will go back into the work of Mercy Ministries around the world.

INTRODUCTION

I woke up on the floor drenched in my own vomit. Looking around the unfamiliar bathroom, I struggled to remember what had happened the night before. Everything was such a blur, and the only clue I had was the empty liquor bottle lying next to me and a small, empty plastic bag.

—Kate

After years of living in an addiction to drugs and alcohol, Kate has finally reached rock bottom. To deal with her dysfunctional family, she abused many different substances in an effort to escape the reality she lived in. Little did she know her way of escape was the doorway to her captivity.

The types and varieties of addiction are endless, but through Christ you can find freedom from anything that is controlling and consuming your life. You may be reading this to gain a better understanding of how to help someone you love that is on this downward spiral, or maybe you are struggling with an addiction and are desperate for answers. There are many people, just like you or someone you know, who are looking for a way out. Many have found the way, and you will read some of their stories.

Since 1983, Mercy Ministries has served thousands of young women from across the country and around the world from varied cultural and economic backgrounds. Young women who come to Mercy Ministries are often facing a combination of difficult circumstances, and many of them have sought prior treatment without successful long-term results, yet they graduate from the Mercy Ministries program truly transformed. They are found attending universities, working in ministries and in corporations, on the mission field, and at home raising families. Our residents are young women who want to change and move beyond their difficult circumstances, yet have never been able to before. But at Mercy Ministries, they find hope.

You can find hope, too. This book was written to give you more understanding of your struggle and help you learn practical ways to acknowledge, identify, and eliminate an addiction from your life. There is hope. There is freedom. There is mercy for addictions.

Chapter One

WHAT IS AN ADDICTION?

*L*iving with an addiction is like walking around every day with an iron ball and chain shackled to your leg. It goes with you everywhere, weighs you down, keeps you from reaching your full potential, and controls your life. Every thought, action, and emotion can be dependent on this burden that you are dragging around. It could be drugs, alcohol, tobacco—anything that is consuming your life and impairing your ability to make rational decisions.

When you are only concerned about getting your needs met, you will find yourself living a miserable life of bondage. Galatians 5:19–21 (MSG) describes what this often looks like:

> *It is obvious what kind of life develops out of trying to get your own way all the time: repetitive, loveless, cheap sex; a stinking accumulation of mental and emotional garbage; frenzied and joyless grabs for happiness; trinket gods; magic-show religion; paranoid loneliness; cutthroat competition; all-consuming-yet-never-satisfied wants; a brutal temper; an impotence to love or be loved; divided homes and divided lives; small-minded and lopsided pursuits; the vicious habit of depersonalizing everyone into a rival; uncontrolled and uncontrollable addictions; ugly parodies of community. I could go on. This isn't the first time I have warned you, you know. If you use your freedom this way, you will not inherit God's kingdom.*

When you cannot function until the demands of the addiction are met, you need to stop and ask yourself if you really want to spend the rest of your life living for the next fix. You may think you have no choice, but you do.

Signs and Symptoms

An addiction goes far beyond the stigmas society places on those who live on the streets, selling their own bodies to get their next "fix." While that scenario is a reality for many who are trapped in an addiction, there are also those who never find freedom because they cannot see the reality of their own destructive actions. Here are a few signs that you or someone you know may be dealing with an addiction:

- Change in personality or tolerance level for people
- Lying, manipulative behaviors
- Significant change in sleeping and eating patterns
- Feeling that you need the substance regularly and, in some cases, intense cravings throughout the day
- Making certain you maintain a supply of the drug
- Doing things to obtain the drug that you normally would never do, such as stealing or prostituting yourself
- Feeling that you need the substance to deal with your problems
- Driving or doing other activities that place you and others at risk of physical harm when you're under the influence
- Inability to fulfill major responsibilities at home, school, or work
- Repeated legal problems because of substance use
- Requiring more of the substance to produce the same effect

- Repeated attempts and failures to limit substance use
- Needing the substance to relieve withdrawal symptoms
- Spending significant time using, recovering from, or obtaining the substance
- Knowing the physical or psychological problems of using, but continuing to use the substance
- Isolating from family

Root Issues

Many root issues may be driving you to these behaviors. One common root behind any addictive behavior is abuse. Whether it is physical, sexual, verbal, or emotional abuse, the overwhelming emotions abuse produces lead a person to find a way to escape the shame, pain, guilt, and anger. For example, you may think you are coping by unwinding with a few drinks, but soon the effects of the alcohol will wear off, leaving you right back where you started.

Living in an environment with family dysfunction may encourage you to survive through temporary means. If the use of alcohol and drugs continues to be the solution, it could eventually be the very thing that destroys you. If your motive is to escape, suppress, or self-medicate, then you are only delaying the healing work God wants to do in your life.

Feelings of shame, anger, hopelessness, sadness, or other intense emotions could come from a variety of circumstances and may leave you with a huge void inside your heart. You may have grabbed the first thing available as a temporary fix, not being sure of what to do, but now you realize your fix has become a seemingly normal part of your daily routine.

No substance on this earth will ever be able to fill the void in your life. There is not a sufficient amount of any physical substance that will bring you the emotional fulfillment your heart desires. There is no pill that will ever heal the pain you feel from the tragedies you have experienced in your life. In fact, relying on a substance or activity to ease your pain will have the opposite effect: You'll be left feeling more hopeless and alone than ever before when you depend on anything other than God.

Only God can heal the pain and release you from the need to turn to these addictive behaviors. His solutions are never temporary, and His truth will leave a permanent impact on your life. When you are running to anything other than God to get your needs met, you will be left empty and disappointed every time.

Wake Up!

Just one time won't hurt anything. I have to do something. . . .

Almost every addiction begins with that lie, and believing it has the power to destroy you. In actuality, one time can hurt you as it triggers a deadly addiction, and one time almost always leads to another.

I tried my first drug when I was twelve and was instantly hooked. I fell very quickly into a deadly downward spiral. After about seven years in the drug world, I was in a hospital room on the brink of death. I almost lost my arm because of the effects of the severe addiction I had to injecting heroin and OxyContin into my veins.

—Amy

Now is the time to trace back and identify the trail of lies you have believed that have left you in the pit of an addiction. Every lie comes from the father of lies—Satan—and you must identify him as the voice you are listening to. Satan is behind anything and everything that is evil on this earth, and he comes only to steal, kill, and destroy all that is good (John 10:10). When you become familiar with God's Word, you will see the perverse nature of the devil and will be able to recognize his voice for what it truly is.

Anytime you hear a lie you are also presented with a choice: You can believe that lie, or you can dismiss it and believe the truth that comes from God. This is clearly presented to you in Deuteronomy 30:19–20 (NLT): "Today I have given you the choice between life and death, between blessings and curses. Now I call on heaven and earth to witness the choice you make. Oh, that you would choose life, so that you and your descendants might live!"

God does not promise you will never be tempted, but He does promise He will always give you a way out. "God is faithful; he will not let you be tempted beyond what you can bear. But when you are tempted, he will also provide a way out so that you can stand up under it" (1 Corinthians 10:13).

There is urgency in God's call for you to rise up out of the addiction that has held you captive. Even though you may feel like no one cares, or that your friends and family have given up on you, God has not, nor will He ever give up on you. He created you. Therefore He sees the incredible potential you have to live a fulfilling life. The following passage in Isaiah 52 is a cry from God, calling you out of captivity!

"Awake, awake, put on your strength, O Zion; put on your beautiful garments. . . . Shake yourself from the dust and arise

. . . loose the bonds from your neck, O captive daughter of Zion" (Isaiah 52:1–2 ESV).

When you are coming off a drug or waking up the morning after you have had too many drinks, the last thing you may want to hear is someone telling you, "Wake up! Shake it off and get up!" These words may sound strong, but God is saying that it's time to be aggressive in getting out of this lifestyle, and you need to do whatever it takes to rise up. He loves you enough to make sure you are aware of the consequences of your actions and that you know you have a choice. When He sees you are serious and determined to turn away from the addiction, He will be there with abounding forgiveness and grace.

Overcome

When you surrender your addiction to Christ and submit your heart to Him, He will give you the ability to overcome the addiction. Grace is divine enablement available in Christ to do what He asks you to do. In 2 Timothy 2, Paul encouraged Timothy to be strong in the grace that is in Christ. Timothy was becoming weak-hearted because of all the things that were coming against him and his calling as an apostolic leader. He was forgetting who he was—an apostle for Christ! But Paul reminded him to stir up the gift that was in him and to be strong in grace—divine enablement, not human strength or effort. Grace is so much more than a free gift. It is supernatural ability that enables us to do what we need to do.

Grace is God's undeserved favor. It is extended out of His endless love and has no limits when you have made the decision to submit your heart and life to God. Grace means that God looks beyond your imperfection and sin, and He loves you despite the wrong you have done.

However, the key to being able to overcome is to have a desire and willingness to change and to turn away from what you are doing. Once you have made the decision to let go of the addiction, then God releases His strength and power to enable you to walk out this decision. He loves you where you are and accepts you where you are, but the change comes once you make the decision to surrender and to turn and go another direction. God releases His power and ability in you to overcome, and He actually changes your desires.

A common misconception about freedom in Christ is that it gives permission to sin. The truth is that His forgiveness is always available, but true freedom means you have a choice. You were once a slave to sin, but now you are given the power to choose not to sin. What you used to be a slave to, you now have the power to walk away from. So, continue to choose freedom; otherwise, you will become entangled again with the same yoke of bondage (Galatians 5:1). Your freedom is not a license to sin, your freedom gives you the power to choose life (Deuteronomy 30:19).

We can look again to the life of the apostle Paul, who explained the purpose of grace and the need to turn away from sin in the following passage:

> *So, since we're out from under the old tyranny, does that mean we can live any old way we want? Since we're free in the freedom of God, can we do anything that comes to mind? Hardly. You know well enough from your own experience that there are some acts of so-called freedom that destroy freedom. Offer yourselves to sin, for instance, and*

it's your last free act. But offer yourselves to the ways of God and the freedom never quits. All your lives you've let sin tell you what to do. But thank God you've started listening to a new master, one whose commands set you free to live openly in his freedom!

—Romans 6:15–18 MSG

Living a life detached from God will not bring freedom, but will lead to a dead-end road of destruction. When you are able to break away from being bound to the cravings and demands of the addiction, you will find the delight of obeying what God tells you to do! "Work hard for sin your whole life and your pension is death. But God's gift is *real life*, eternal life, delivered by Jesus, our Master" (Romans 6:23 MSG).

I saw my parents as being too overprotective and resented them for never giving me enough freedom. I began to rebel as a preteen and would sneak out of the house at night with my friends to get high. I felt so free—like I was finally able to do whatever I wanted. I was lying all the time, and after a while, my parents noticed that something was going on. I lied to cover more lies until the only thing left was to run away. I moved in with my boyfriend, who was a dealer, and even though I could do whatever I wanted, I never felt as trapped as I did then. My boyfriend was abusive and manipulative, and I never felt safe with him. I couldn't leave him because I couldn't afford the drugs without him. This was not what I thought freedom would be like.

—Kayla

God will take your mess and turn it into a message if you will just choose to step out of the mess and allow God to do

His redemptive work. Every choice you will make in life will affect four areas: your family, your friends, your future, and your relationship with God. It is important to remember that what you do does not only affect you. Thankfully, God's grace is so amazing that He will wipe your slate clean, and He promises to restore all that was lost in any of these areas!

Chapter Two
BREAKING FREE

*O*nce you have decided you are tired of living with an addiction and truly desire freedom, you may be unsure of what to do next. Realizing you have a problem is a huge first step, but often the next step can be just as difficult. You have to realize that you cannot do this alone. An addiction is bigger than you and requires more than just willpower to break free.

God is the only one who knows you better than you know yourself. He has seen everything you have done and experienced, and He still loves you enough to set you free. Jesus Christ paid the ultimate sacrifice for your freedom. He endured ridicule, mockery, rejection, and cruel torture that led to His death on the cross. The unbelievable thing is that He didn't do anything to deserve this. He chose to bear the punishment on your behalf in order to give you a life of freedom.

Satan would love for you to believe you are still a slave to addiction. But the truth is, at the cross it was finished! Jesus took on the sin of the world so you could be free. It is time to expose the lie and receive the truth so you can walk free and live a new life.

Surrender your heart to God and become familiar with His voice so you can break the cycle of addiction in your life. When you allow God to heal the pain of your past and walk you through the process of withdrawal, you will break free from the addiction as you continue to renew your mind with the truth of God's Word.

These ideas may seem foreign or even scary at first, but until the pain of staying the same becomes greater than the pain of change, you will never change. This is not the easy way out, but it is the only way. You may walk through a tough period of time feeling like you will never make it through, but keep your focus and know it's worth the fight! You have to push past the temporary pain to experience eternal freedom. What will it take for you to realize you are ready for change?

Surrender Your Heart

When you surrender your heart, you are letting go of your own plans, your own agendas, and your own will. You are acknowledging that you cannot break free on your own, and you cannot continue to live in daily torment. God knows and sees everything, but it is vital that you recognize His presence in your life and surrender your heart to Him. He is a loving, patient God and will not force Himself into your life. He will wait until you see that only through Him will you be able to experience the freedom, love, joy, and peace you're searching for, and that only by accepting His will for your life will you know the incredible plans He has for you. Jeremiah 29:11 says, "'For I know the plans I have for you,' declares the LORD, 'plans to prosper you and not to harm you, plans to give you hope and a future.'"

On the cross, Jesus willingly gave His life for you. In that surrender, He equipped you with the same power to surrender your life. Philippians 4:13 says, "I can do everything through him who gives me strength." When you accept Jesus into your heart and allow Him to be the Lord of your life, you start over with a completely clean slate. He separates your sins as far as the east is from the west and will hold nothing against you (Psalm 103:12). There is nothing too great for God's forgiveness, and there is nothing His grace doesn't cover. Any voice telling you God could not forgive you, or that you are the one exception after what you have done, is lying! Quickly identify this lying voice as the enemy's, who would love for you to accept failure and refuse to invite Jesus into your heart and life.

You may have fallen into an addiction after you already accepted Jesus as your Lord and Savior, but again, God's grace and forgiveness is endless. As you submit to God's will and commit your life to Him, you will be a threat to the enemy and his evil schemes. He is looking only to steal from, kill, and destroy you.

It is ultimately your choice, and you must ask yourself, "Do I want death, or do I want life?" If you choose Christ, you choose the abundant life He brings. Here is an example of a prayer you can pray to ask Jesus to come into your heart. He has been patiently waiting for you—all you have to do is ask.

Prayer for Salvation

Jesus, I am at the end of my rope and am tired of trying to survive on my own. I have made such a mess of my life, and I thank you that you died on the cross to set me free from the prison I have created for myself. I believe you are the Son of God, and I believe you died on a cross for my sin and shame. I know it will not always be easy, but with you I will never be alone. This day, I choose life. I choose you. I ask you to come into my heart and to be Lord of my life. I want you to be in charge. I know you will walk with me on this journey, so I will rest in knowing you will help me through it all. In Jesus' name, Amen.

If you just prayed this prayer with a sincere heart, you are now a child of God with an incredible inheritance in the Kingdom of God as you choose to walk in obedience to Him. When you receive Jesus as your Savior, you inherit eternal life in heaven and are saved from an eternity in hell. Life begins the moment you experience salvation. Jesus died a horrible death on the cross and was buried in a tomb, but He didn't stay there! Three days later, He rose from the dead and demanded the keys to death, hell, and the grave so He could extend freedom to you. His death not only brings forgiveness, but also secures an eternal life of freedom as you choose to walk in it. If you just prayed this prayer of salvation, that life starts right now for you!

Listen to God's Voice

After His death and resurrection, Jesus stayed on the earth only a short time before He ascended into heaven. When He left, He sent the Holy Spirit to help guide and direct you on the right path. He promised,

> *When the Spirit of truth comes, He will guide you into all truth. He will not speak on His own but will tell you what He has heard. He will tell you about the future. He will bring me glory by telling you whatever He receives from me. All that belongs to the Father is mine; this is why I said, "The Spirit will tell you whatever He receives from me."*
>
> —John 16:13–15 NLT

According to these verses, you have the ability to hear from God without having to go through anyone else. Yes, God will often use others to speak truth into your life or give you a word of direction and encouragement, but God also speaks directly to your heart if you are willing to listen. This is rarely an audible voice, but a quiet inner voice that gently guides you according to God's Word. It is important to find a mature Christian friend or mentor who can teach you how to use God's Word.

God will never tell you to do something that goes against what He has written in His Word. For example, if you are in a store and you think God is saying you deserve to have that shirt and you should just take it without paying because you really need it, you will see in the Bible that God says stealing is wrong. It also says that as His child you are to trust Him, knowing He will provide all of your needs because He loves you.

The more you read God's Word, the more familiar you will become with His voice. John 10:4 (AB) says, "When he has brought his own sheep outside, he walks on before them, and the sheep follow him because they know his voice." Once you can clearly recognize God's voice, you will also be able to recognize the voice of the enemy and steer clear of his destructive path.

Break the Cycle

The choices you make can result in life or death for you, but they also can bring life and death to the generations that will follow you. Addiction is a pattern that is often repeated and passed on from generation to generation. Take a look down your family line. Do you notice any patterns or a history in your family with addictions?

God promises blessings when you choose to obey His Word, but disobedience will only lead to more heartache in your life, as well as in the lives of your children and grandchildren. The good news is that Jesus gives you the authority to break that cycle that has been destroying your family so you do not have to live bound by the wrong choices that were made long before your time!

Take time to identify the issues in your family. A few examples are depression, anger, addictions, pride, sexual sins, abuse, fear, manipulation, and emotional dependency. Once you have identified the struggles, ask God to break these patterns and sins in your life and the lives of your descendants. Jesus has given you the authority to break these curses from previous generations so you can pass on blessings instead.

Prayer to Break Generational Patterns

Father God, I thank you that I do not have to live a life of addictions patterned after the generations of my family. I thank you that through Jesus Christ, I have the authority to break this cycle of addiction in my own life, and prevent it from affecting my children and grandchildren. In Jesus' name, I ask you to break any and all harmful and sinful generational patterns in my family. I choose to forgive my parents and ancestors, releasing any feelings of bitterness or resentment for the consequences their sin had on my life. I ask you to forgive me for giving in to temptation and yielding to the sin. I receive your forgiveness and choose to move forward. I will no longer live under the cloak of shame for my wrong choices. In Jesus' name, Amen.

Release Past Pain

When you started reading this book, you may have identified some root issues in your life that have led you on the path to an addiction. You might have experienced abuse, been hurt emotionally, felt rejected or abandoned by someone you trusted, or had to grieve the death of a loved one. Your life does not have to be controlled by the pain of your past. When you expose your heart to God and allow Him into those deep and painful places in your life, He will heal your heart and set you free from the heavy burdens you were never meant to carry.

In Matthew 11:28 (NLT) Jesus said, "Come to me, all of you who are weary and carry heavy burdens, and I will give you rest." You may have been living in a self-survival mode, feeling like you have to take care of yourself, deal with your own pain, and not trust anyone along the way. God not only listens to your heart and heals your wounds, but He will teach you how to live. God is trustworthy. He will relieve you of your burdens as you lay them down at the feet of Jesus. It is time to let the addiction go!

Part of letting go of the past is making a choice to forgive those who have hurt you. Forgiveness is not a feeling or emotion. Forgiveness does not justify the sin that was committed against you, but it does release you to receive God's forgiveness in your own life. Jesus said, "For if you forgive men when they sin against you, your heavenly Father will also forgive you. But if you do not forgive men their sins, your Father will not forgive your sins" (Matthew 6:14–15).

When you forgive those who have hurt you, God removes your burden of feeling like you have to protect and defend yourself, and He steps into that role for you as your vindicator. He promises,

"And I will deal severely with all who have oppressed you. I will save the weak and helpless ones" (Zephaniah 3:19 NLT).

God doesn't come into your life to free you from just a few things. He wants you to experience complete healing and restoration, which includes freedom from unforgiveness. Unforgiveness leads to bitterness and resentment and can then turn into anger and rage. The only person you are hurting by holding a grudge is yourself! Unforgiveness is a huge hindrance to your relationship with God and will keep you from receiving all God has for you, including forgiveness for your own sins.

God desires more than anything to have a relationship with you. He wants to be your Lord and Savior, Protector and Provider, but also your Friend and Father. If your earthly father abused or abandoned you, you may have a distorted perception of God. But God is so much more than even the best earthly father could ever be. God is a *perfect* father.

Reading the Bible will help you to learn the characteristics of God and to avoid basing your perception of God on what you know from earthly relationships. Do not let the shame of what you have done keep you from approaching God. Know that He truly understands the struggle of what you are going through.

Hebrews 4:15 (NCV) says, "For our high priest is able to understand our weaknesses. He was tempted in every way that we are, but he did not sin." Jesus is our example, and you have to trust that you can release your pain to Him and allow Him to carry your burdens for you. Come boldly before His throne in your time of need, knowing that He is moved with compassion toward our humanity. Just surrender control to Him, and He will give you rest! Here is an example of a prayer you can pray in your time of need:

Prayer to Release Past Pain

Dear Jesus, I choose to forgive those who have hurt me, and I receive your forgiveness from the sins I have committed against others out of my own pain. I thank you, Lord, that you are so gracious to me and are willing to come into my heart and heal the pain of my past experiences. Thank you for the freedom and healing you are bringing into my life as I choose to forgive and for revealing to my heart your true character so that I can have a relationship with you. In Jesus' name I pray, Amen.

Withdrawal

One of our key staff members at Mercy Ministries went through a very rough time many years ago, struggling with a six-year addiction to drugs. She was so trapped that she even resorted to selling her body to maintain her addiction. Despite her anger at God, she eventually reached the point that she knew she had to run back to God or she was going to die. She has now been on staff at Mercy Ministries for fourteen years and plays a key role every day in helping other young women around the world find freedom from life-controlling issues. This is her story.

I can remember how scared I was at the whole idea of withdrawing from so much stuff in my system. It was hard enough when I couldn't get to my drugs fast enough and would begin to feel the shakes, headache, and pain coming on. There were times when just the idea of it going much further would nearly scare me to death. I thought I really would die.

I had been addicted to drugs and alcohol for about three years when I realized that I had pretty much sold or lost everything that meant anything to me, and I still didn't have enough money to keep up my habits. I decided that all I had left was to sell my body in exchange for what made life bearable for me: drugs, alcohol, and numbness to life itself. I hated living. I tried to kill myself, but someone found me in time to stop the process. That really made me all the more mad at God because I didn't have any reason to live, but He wouldn't let me die. What kind of God was He, anyway? I hated Him, and I made sure He knew it every day.

After being on drugs and alcohol and selling my body for more than six years, I came to another realization: I was still miserable. I couldn't seem to get enough drugs, alcohol, or sex to drown out the pain and anger, and I didn't have the strength to keep it all up any longer. The thought of giving my life back to God when I hated Him so much was almost as miserable a thought to me, but I really didn't know what else to do. I knew this meant the whole withdrawal process was imminent and unavoidable.

I didn't go back to God with tears of repentance; I went back in anger and defeat, knowing I couldn't make it without Him. I threw my life at Him and told Him if He thought He could do anything with the trashcan life I had, then He could have at it. It wasn't long before I knew He had taken me up on the offer. It doesn't matter how you come to Him, it only matters that you come to Him.

The symptoms of withdrawal came, and I figured I would either die in that process, finally ending my rollercoaster life, or I would make it through somehow to something better. Anything would have been better at that point.

I remember so many times I would wobble into the kitchen of my parents' home, holding on to the counter so I wouldn't fall down. The shakes would come on so badly, and I could feel my tongue get thick. My dad would stand behind me and my mom in front. They would lock their arms together around me and hold on while I jerked and convulsed. I could hear them praying the whole time, but it sounded far away until the seizure would pass. I spent several days this way; and when we all look back on it now, we realize we were running a horrific risk by not taking me to professionals for help. It was God's grace that brought us through that time, and I now know that very clearly.

I wish the story ended there, but that is really where it just began. I spent the next year trying to find clarity in my thought life again. There were times of loneliness that drove me to go back to my old friends and the familiar drink or snort of hash. Sometimes I would give in to an old lover and go back to my parents' house wearing a new and yet old familiar shame. But God kept loving me, and He kept showing me He was there and that I didn't have to keep going backward to get ahead in life.

The day I decided that no matter what, I would not go back to anything or anyone of the past was the day something broke off me. It was like an invisible line had been drawn in the sand. I was on one side and my old life was on the other. I somehow knew in my heart that if I ever crossed over again I would never find my way back to God and to hope. I still felt very crippled by everything that started the process of not wanting to feel or think, but I simultaneously felt for the first time that I would walk out of that emotional wheelchair and be alright. I also know that only God gives that to someone who has gone so far away from Him on purpose.

I remember my first worship service at the church when I was clearheaded and could really listen to the words of the songs and think about their meaning. I wept. There were torrents of tears that fell that day, and God began to wash away the pain. Every time I remembered something painful, I would lift it up in my hands during worship or prayer, and I would feel God taking my brokenness like an offering. I didn't understand that kind of love and don't know that I ever fully will. I only know that it is real and that I am healed.

—Mary

Mary's decision to recommit her life to Christ was the beginning of turning her life around, but it was not easy. She went through a very difficult time of withdrawal because of what she had done to her body.

In my twenty-five-plus years of working with addictions, I have seen God supernaturally deliver people from addictions and withdrawal symptoms. However, in my experience, this is not the norm. There is no question that God has the power to deliver—He can and will deliver. It is my personal opinion, however, that God may allow you to go through the pain and consequences so you can remember how difficult it was the next time you are tempted to go back to that same bondage. Hopefully, the thought of experiencing the agony of withdrawal again will cause you to think twice about turning back to substance abuse.

Making a total commitment of your life to Christ and running to God for help is the starting point, but it is only the beginning. Transformation is a process, and you have to change the way you think if you want to change the way you act. If you want to be transformed on the inside, you have to begin to identify with who you are in Christ and not what you used to be in your past.

As I have already stated, it is important to think and talk about yourself in terms of being a new creation in Christ instead of being a "recovering drug addict." Identifying with the past gives your past power over you; whereas, identifying with who you are in Christ releases the power of God in your life to overcome anything you may face.

It is extremely important that during the time you are learning to walk in your new life, you have people around you who will hold you accountable. Part of what makes Mercy Ministries such a successful program is the constant accountability girls experience around the clock as they are taught principles to walk out their new life.

Here is an example of a prayer to help you through this time.

Prayer to Press Through

Dear Jesus, I thank you that your strength is perfected in my weakness and that when I am weak, you are strong. What I am going through is so hard, and there are days when I'm not sure I'm going to make it, but I know that what I'm feeling and experiencing is only temporary.

I thank you that as I press through the pain, you are bringing me into a life that is free from the bondage of addiction. In Jesus' name I pray, Amen.

Be Transformed

One of the greatest abuses of power in the medical and mental health industries involves certain doctors, psychiatrists, and counselors who are licensed to write prescriptions for psychotropic medications. Sometimes professionals will charge large amounts of money to listen to your problem and then give you a prescription for a drug, saying you have a chemical imbalance.

If you are going to a doctor who is giving you mood-elevating drugs or psychotropic medications, you need to consider if the medication is truly needed or if you are running from dealing with the root issues. You need to first deal with the inner turmoil by inviting Jesus Christ into your life, and then you need to put the Word of God in your heart and mind. Ask God to change you from the inside out, because medicating your problems only treats the symptoms. You might feel better for a while, but medication alone will not heal you or release you from the pain of your addiction. Only God can do that.

If someone tells you that you're a "recovering alcoholic" or a "recovering drug addict," that is a lie. If you have accepted Jesus Christ as your Savior and the Lord of your life, 2 Corinthians 5:17 says in Christ you are "a new creature. Old things have passed away and all things are new." You are not "recovering" from anything! If that were true, then the apostle Paul needed to be in a group for recovering murderers and the apostle Peter would need to be in a group for recovering liars.

Please understand this: Old things have really and truly passed away and all things are new. Your past is just that—your past. The old is dead, the new has come, and your past does not have to destroy your future. You are a new creature, and you can do just like the apostle Paul did: "But one thing I do: Forgetting what is behind and straining toward what is ahead, I press on toward the goal to win the prize for which God has called me heavenward in Christ Jesus" (Philippians 3:13–14). You are the righteousness of God in Jesus Christ (2 Corinthians 5:21). God has not given you a spirit of fear, but of power and love and of a sound mind (2 Timothy 1:7). Renew your mind to that!

The power of the gospel of Jesus Christ is in its simplicity. If it is not simple enough for a child to understand, then it is too complicated. But somewhere along the line, people have tried to complicate it, inserting their intellect and reasoning. Now, I'm not suggesting that you shouldn't go to school, get a degree, and pursue knowledge and higher learning. In fact, I encourage you to do so. But any time a person exalts academic degrees and the knowledge of man over the wisdom of God, that person is actually acting as though he thinks he's smarter than God.

There are certainly health care professionals out there who know and love the Lord, but you have to search for them. They're not impressed by their own degrees and experience, but simply use them as tools to bring the greater truth, which is freedom in Christ. And they know a prescription doesn't bring healing. Only God can do that. Find professionals who believe this way and connect with them. 1 Corinthians 1:19, 26–31 says,

> *I will destroy the wisdom of the wise; the intelligence of the*
> *intelligent I will frustrate . . . . Brothers, think of what*
> *you were when you were called. Not many of you were wise*

by human standards; not many were influential; not many were of noble birth. But God chose the foolish things of the world to shame the wise; God chose the weak things of the world to shame the strong. He chose the lowly things of this world and the despised things—and the things that are not—to nullify the things that are, so that no one may boast before him. It is because of him that you are in Christ Jesus, who has become for us wisdom from God—that is, our righteousness, holiness and redemption. Therefore, as it is written: "Let him who boasts boast in the Lord."

It doesn't matter what the problem is, we have the answer—His name is Jesus! Proverbs 3:5–6 says, "Trust in the LORD with all your heart and lean not on your own understanding; in all your ways acknowledge him, and he will make your paths straight."

Speak the Truth

Reading the Bible is a good thing—a necessary thing—but there is power when you speak the Word of God out loud. The Bible says your tongue and the words you speak actually have the power of life and death (Proverbs 18:21). Knowing this should lead you to think before you speak something negative about someone else, but most importantly, it should encourage you to speak the truth of God's Word over your life.

You may be believing many lies about yourself every day that determine your actions, thoughts, and emotions. It is important to identify the lies so you can replace them with the truth from God's Word. You must address the lies you believe, because these negative thoughts will determine your emotions, and your emotions usually determine your behaviors.

As you continue to read the Bible and know more and more truth, you will gradually understand what areas of your life need to be changed. For example, if you believe you are and always will be an addict, your actions will be a reflection of that belief, and you will remain a victim to that mentality. God's Word says you are a new creation in Christ, and that means that anyone who belongs to Christ has become a new person. The old life is gone and a new life has begun (2 Corinthians 5:17). You are no longer bound by that old identity. You now have a new identity, and it's important to begin to identify with the fact that you have been made new in Christ. Instead of saying, "I am a recovering addict," begin to declare over your life (yes, speak it out loud!) something like this: "Lord, your Word says in 2 Corinthians 5:17 that old things have passed away and all things are new. I thank you that I am a new creation in Christ." There are more examples of truths from God's Word to replace the lies you may believe in the appendix of this book.

During the times you feel the weakest, remember that you can still be strong because God promises that His strength is perfected in your weakness (2 Corinthians 12:9). Don't be afraid to cry out to God and reach out to supportive people to help you get through this difficult time. It is necessary to have a strong support system. You may even need to stay with someone temporarily for extra accountability. Choose someone who will encourage you to walk in truth and who knows how to pray. When you feel like you have no strength and you cannot make it another moment without giving in to the struggle, allow your support team and prayer partners to carry you. Begin speaking the things you know are truth and stand in faith that the God who died for you will bring you through!

Chapter Three

STAYING FREE

God provides you with the principles necessary to break free, and He equips you with tools that will allow you to maintain your freedom. Freedom in Christ is not about a set of rules or restrictions. Instead, it's a set of boundaries that keeps you from falling back into the grip of sin.

God gives us boundaries and directs us in the same way a parent directs her child into the safety of a backyard and away from a busy street. The parent's intent is not to be harsh or controlling, but to protect her child. In the same way, your heavenly Father wants to guide and protect you. You have complete freedom to play, enjoy life, and have fun, but He will show you where the boundaries are to keep you safe. God gives the wonderful gift of choice for good, but He offers guidelines to keep us from what would be harmful to us.

God will never force you to obey Him, but know that it is through your obedience that you will find freedom. God's boundary lines are there for your protection, not restriction. When you are tempted, remember the pain of your past so you won't go there again.

"Christ has set us free to live a free life. So take your stand! Never again let anyone put a harness of slavery on you" (Galatians 5:1 MSG). You will need to make intentional choices to surround yourself with like-minded people who will be spiritually supportive and also hold you accountable. You'll also need to conform your life to God's Word so He can change your desires (Romans 12:2). Continue speaking God's Word over your life, and pursue the incredible life that God has for you. Embrace your identity in Christ, and you will stay free from the bondage of an addiction.

Be Intentional

Breaking free from an addiction usually involves a complete lifestyle change, which may involve many practical adjustments in your daily life. Please take the time to find a good local church and get connected with someone who can mentor you through this healing process—do not try to do it alone! What you're doing is much like venturing into a whole new world, and at first you may feel very uncomfortable. Adjusting to this new life will take time—finding new hobbies, making different friends—but it will be so worth it in the end!

During this time you must be very cautious and intentional about your choices regarding who you spend your time with, where you go, and what you choose to think about. Stay very close to the guidance of God's Word. Proverbs 4:25–27 says, "Let your eyes look straight ahead, fix your gaze directly before you. Make level paths for your feet and take only ways that are firm. Do not swerve to the right or the left; keep your foot from evil." This verse means that you have to stay alert and aware of the consequences of your actions.

Before you think about walking into a bar, even without the intention of drinking, you must ask yourself if you are stepping into a place that may cause you to stumble back into a temptation. When you are making plans to hang out with old friends you must ask yourself, "Are they going to be doing or talking about things that will cause me to fall back into my old patterns?" If the answer is yes, then it would be wise to reconsider your plans. Making compulsive decisions is not wise and will land you in a situation that could compromise your freedom. You have to be honest about the areas where you are weak and avoid situations or relationships that would cause you to compromise.

God will never put you in a situation or allow you to be faced with more than you can handle, but you can put yourself in a compromising position by making bad choices. Use common sense, which will mean walking away from the places of temptation—or maybe even running away!

The friends around you might not understand why you don't want to do the things you used to do, but you may soon become an example to them as they watch you living in freedom from that addiction. Until then, know that God is your provider, and He will provide healthy, godly relationships in your life to encourage you and speak truth.

Do not fear that choosing to follow God's plan will cause you to live a life that is miserable and lonely, even though you may go through periods where loneliness may feel overwhelming. Know that God is faithful, and He will place people around you who can show you what relationships are really supposed to look like. Learning to cope with changes in life patterns is essential in overcoming loneliness. This is why you have to be very intentional about reaching out to others and be willing to form new relationships.

Relationships based on addiction often center around self-gratification. However, as you begin to step out of your comfort zone and meet new people, God will reveal the true meaning of selfless relationships through those around you. "Love is patient and kind. Love is not jealous or boastful or proud or rude. It does not demand its own way. It is not irritable, and it keeps no record of being wronged. It does not rejoice about injustice but rejoices whenever the truth wins out. Love never gives up, never loses faith, is always hopeful, and endures through every circumstance" (1 Corinthians 13:4–7 NLT).

People whose lives are rooted in the love of Christ should be your constant companions. Remember, you become like the people you hang out with! The choice is yours.

Stand Firm

The battle for your life does not stop when you receive Jesus as your Savior. Every day when you wake up and begin your day, you are entering the battlefield. For a soldier, entering the battlefield without any armor on would be absurd, and the same is true for you. Ephesians 6:11 (NLT) says to "Put on all of God's armor so that you will be able to stand firm against all strategies of the devil." The Bible goes on to list the elements of the armor you should be putting on every day:

> *Therefore, put on every piece of God's armor so you will be able to resist the enemy in the time of evil. Then after the battle, you will still be standing firm. Stand your ground, putting on the belt of truth and the body armor of God's righteousness. For shoes, put on the peace that comes from the Good News so that you will be fully prepared. In addition to all of these, hold up the shield of faith to stop the fiery arrows of the devil. Put on salvation as your helmet, and take the sword of the Spirit, which is the word of God.*
> *—Ephesians 6:12–17 NLT*

To help you better understand the armor of God and what it means, I want to teach you how to practically apply this to your life.

The helmet of salvation represents the mind of Christ, which you receive when you ask Jesus into your heart. As you renew your mind by reading God's Word, you are placing a symbolic helmet on your head that helps you think the right thoughts and protects your mind from the onslaughts of the enemy. As you bring every thought captive to Christ, then you are able to change the way you think about your situation and about life. You will begin to think of yourself as an overcomer.

The breastplate of righteousness symbolizes the exchange that happens when you ask Jesus into your life: You give Him your sin, mistakes, and addictions, and He gives you His righteousness or right standing with God.

2 Corinthians 5:21 explains that Jesus, who had no sin, became sin for you so you can now receive His righteousness. In other words, you can actually exchange your sins and mistakes for God's righteousness—which means that you are now in right standing with God!

Because of your standing, or position, when thoughts and feelings of self-condemnation and self-hate come at you, you can refuse them and say, "*No!* I am a new creation!" Understanding this righteousness protects you from the destructive thought patterns that will lead you down a dead-end street—back to old habits and behaviors.

Wearing the belt of truth means that you choose to conform your life to God's Word and you choose to walk in His principles. By walking in truth, you automatically leave deception behind. For example, when you are walking north, your back is turned to the south and you are literally walking away from the south.

Similarly, when you choose to do the right thing, you don't have to worry about doing the wrong thing because wrong is automatically eliminated by doing right. In fact, the word *repent* in the Bible means to turn around and go the opposite direction (Acts 3:19).

To wear the shoes of peace means that when you receive Christ as your Savior, you also receive His peace, which will guard your heart and mind. "God's peace, which exceeds anything we can understand" (Philippians 4:7 NLT), will be given to you so you don't have to live in turmoil anymore. Therefore, when you put on the shoes of peace, you are walking and living in peace instead of walking and living in turmoil and chaos.

When you take the shield of faith, which quenches every fiery dart of the wicked one, it means that your faith is now in God and that you trust Him as you live the way He wants you to live. It means that you use the faith God has given you to live for Him and that you truly believe what His Word says. God's Word allows you to deflect the arrows of assault, fear, and doubt that the enemy shoots at you.

The first five pieces of armor are for your protection, but the last piece is an offensive weapon called the sword of the Spirit. To use the sword of the Spirit is to literally speak God's Word out loud. God promises that as you declare and decree His Word, He will watch over His Word to perform it. When Satan came to tempt Jesus (Matthew 4), Jesus responded with "It is written . . ." which is exactly what you need to do.

For example, when you start hearing the voice that says you will never overcome, you can respond with Philippians 4:13 (NLT): "I can do everything through Christ, who gives me strength" or Luke 18:27 (NLT): "What is impossible for people is possible with God."

This is why it is so important to know the Word of God. You need to be able to speak the Word of God as your weapon. Hebrews 4:12 says the sword of the Spirit, the Word of God, is sharper than any double-edged sword, and it has the ability to discern between that which is good and that which is evil, that which is right and that which is wrong. When you stand firm with the armor God gives you, you will be fully protected, and you will win every time.

Drive Out Deception

The best way to counteract a natural tendency to lie is to practice rigorous honesty. You must think before you speak, making sure the words that you are about to say are based only on truth. This also includes any type of exaggeration or manipulation. You may have to go to some people and ask for forgiveness to come clean about a lie that you may have told them. You will feel so free when you no longer have to worry about covering up your lies and when you are able to let go of living a double life. When you walk away from honesty, you are stepping back into bondage. Remember, you have to drive out deception with truth!

Redirect Your Passions

With my focus set on only one thing, I was willing to do whatever it took to get what I wanted. I was working overtime and somehow could never pay my rent on time or keep my electricity on for more than a few weeks. All of my money went to my drugs. I put my child in very dangerous situations, leaving her with neighbors I didn't even know, and not picking her up for days on end. I felt hopeless and apathetic about life. I was slowly being consumed by my own obsession.

—Hillary

The path to an addiction requires passion. Your passion to get your needs met through an addiction may have led you to take some extremely drastic measures. Addictions by nature are very deceptive. You may have contrived some outrageous lies, but lying can only continue for so long. When you find yourself trapped by your own lies, the only way out is to remove yourself from relationships. The passion to get your next fix may have led you to sell your personal possessions for drug money, or even prostitute your own body. The question is not whether you have passion, but where are you directing your passion?

God created you to have passion so you could fulfill the purpose He has for you. Jeremiah 1:5 says, "Before I formed you in the womb I knew you, before you were born I set you apart; I appointed you as a prophet to the nations." The destiny God has for you is greater than you can imagine. The enemy knows God created you with incredible potential, so the only way for Satan to keep you from fulfilling your destiny is to redirect your passion to something that will destroy you.

God reveals the schemes of the enemy so you can rise above them. When you are passionate about your selfish desires, you will be left empty, lacking, and incomplete. The answer is to redirect your passions from pursuing self-gratification to pursuing God.

"'Then you will call upon me and come and pray to me, and I will listen to you. You will seek me and find me when you seek me with all your heart. I will be found by you,' declares the LORD" (Jeremiah 29:12–14). The word *seek* does not mean to casually look for something but to passionately pursue it! When you put your whole heart into seeking the Lord, the result is peace and joy, being able to live a life of truth and not have to walk through life paranoid and trapped by your own lies.

When God promises in the Bible to restore all that the enemy stole from you, He means *all* that the enemy stole from you. 1 Peter 5:10 says, "In his kindness God called you to share in his eternal glory by means of Christ Jesus. So after you have suffered a little while, he will restore, support, and strengthen you, and he will place you on a firm foundation." This includes the passions that became distorted in your life as they led you into an addiction.

When you read the Bible you will find the truth about who you are, and you will develop a relationship with God. He is not a God who is distant or distracted. He wants to be an active part of your daily life. He wants to communicate with you and be involved in your daily decisions, thoughts, and plans. When you learn to walk through your day surrendering your will to His, you will see that His only plan for you is to give you a hope and a future (Jeremiah 29:11)! God will restore a spark of life to your heart, and you will experience the passion God created you to have for a lifetime.

When you redirect your passions and seek the Lord with all your heart, you will find rest, safety, security, and joy; and you will not only know unconditional love, but you will be able to extend it to others. You will find that when you seek God's desires, He will lovingly give you the desires of your heart.

Embrace Who You Are

Even though you may have spent years believing lies about who you are, now is the time to look to God's Word for the truth and make a choice to believe it. Just as a child eagerly accepts all the presents under the Christmas tree with her name on them, so you—with childlike faith—can receive the gifts of truth that God wants to give you.

Jesus said in Matthew 18:3, "I tell you the truth, unless you change and become like little children, you will never enter the kingdom of heaven." Children are so willing to accept truth and therefore are able to inherit God's blessings. God wants you not only to accept truth, but to enthusiastically embrace it as your identity. Nothing you have done or could ever do can separate you from the truth of who God says you are. God's forgiveness and grace are endless, but to receive them, you must submit your heart to God and commit your life to follow His will!

Below you'll see some truths about your true identity in Christ. Practice saying them out loud as you renew your mind with God's Word.

- **I am a child of God.** "To all who believed him and accepted him, he gave the right to become children of God" (John 1:12 NLT).
- **I am the light of the world.** "You are the light of the world— like a city on a hilltop that cannot be hidden" (Matthew 5:14 NLT).
- **I am a joint heir with Christ.** "Since we are his children, we are his heirs. In fact, together with Christ we are heirs of God's glory" (Romans 8:17 NLT).
- **I am a temple, a dwelling place of God.** "Don't you realize that your body is the temple of the Holy Spirit, who lives in you and was given to you by God?" (1 Corinthians 6:19 NLT).

- **I am a new creation.** "Anyone who belongs to Christ has become a new person. The old life is gone; a new life has begun!" (2 Corinthians 5:17 NLT).

- **I am righteous and holy.** "Put on your new nature, created to be like God—truly righteous and holy" (Ephesians 4:24 NLT).

- **I am a threat to the devil.** "I have given you authority to trample on snakes and scorpions and to overcome all the power of the enemy; nothing will harm you" (Luke 10:19).

- **I am free from condemnation.** "There is no condemnation for those who belong to Christ Jesus" (Romans 8:1 NLT).

- **I may approach God with confidence.** "Because of Christ and our faith in him, we can now come boldly and confidently into God's presence" (Ephesians 3:12 NLT).

- **I am complete in Christ.** "You also are complete through your union with Christ, who is the head over every ruler and authority" (Colossians 2:10 NLT).

- **I have been redeemed and forgiven from all of my sins.** "He has rescued us from the kingdom of darkness and transferred us into the Kingdom of his dear Son, who purchased our freedom and forgave our sins" (Colossians 1:13–14 NLT).

- **I am of the light and no longer belong to the darkness.** "You are all sons of the light and sons of the day. We do not belong to the night or to the darkness" (1 Thessalonians 5:5).

- **I am chosen.** "For you are a people holy to the LORD your God. The LORD your God has chosen you out of all the peoples on the face of the earth to be his people, his treasured possession" (Deuteronomy 7:6).

- **I am beautiful and flawless.** "All beautiful you are, my darling; there is no flaw in you" (Song of Songs 4:7).

- **I have peace.** "The LORD gives strength to his people; the LORD blesses his people with peace" (Psalm 29:11).

- **I am accepted.** "Accept one another, then, just as Christ accepted you, in order to bring praise to God" (Romans 15:7).

- **I am a more than a conqueror.** "In all these things we are more than conquerors through him who loved us" (Romans 8:37).

- **I am confident and fearless.** "For God has not given us a spirit of fear and timidity, but of power, love, and self-discipline" (2 Timothy 1:7 NLT).

- **I am treasured.** "For you are a people holy to the LORD your God. The LORD your God has chosen you out of all the peoples on the face of the earth to be his people, his treasured possession" (Deuteronomy 7:6).

- **I am worthy of His love.** "They will walk with me, dressed in white, for they are worthy" (Revelation 3:4).

- **I am a delight to God.** "For the LORD takes delight in his people" (Psalm 149:4).

- **I am secure.** "Let the beloved of the LORD rest secure in him, for he shields him all day long, and the one the LORD loves rests between his shoulders" (Deuteronomy 33:12).

- **I am loved unconditionally.** "Neither height nor depth, nor anything else in all creation, will be able to separate us from the love of God that is in Christ Jesus our Lord" (Romans 8:39).

- **I am gifted.** "We have different gifts, according to the grace given us" (Romans 12:6).

- **I am created in the image of God.** "God created human beings in his own image" (Genesis 1:27 NLT).

- **I am a citizen of heaven.** "But we are citizens of heaven, where the Lord Jesus Christ lives. And we are eagerly waiting for him to return as our Savior" (Philippians 3:20 NLT).

God does not see you according to what you have done, but He sees you through the blood of Jesus, which has covered all your sins. Because of His sacrifice, your past is no longer held against you. Choose to release your past and embrace your true identity in *Him*. Forgiving yourself is the hardest thing to do, and it is a choice. Your feelings may take time to line up, but making that choice to stay in an attitude of forgiveness is imperative to breaking free and staying free from an addiction.

Chapter Four

STORIES OF MERCY

God provides freedom and healing to His children so they can extend the same hope they received from the Lord to others who are in pain and bondage. Angela and Monica have made the choice to break free from the bondage of addiction. As they allowed God access to their broken hearts, they were able to experience personally the incredible freedom only He can bring. They became entangled in the devastation of an addiction but have made the decision to rise above their past and release their pain to God. He is the only one who can turn your story into a testimony of His grace.

As you read these stories of mercy, I pray you will be filled with hope and encouraged that God has a purpose and plan for you beyond your pain and despite the evil plans of the enemy. "But the Lord's plans stand firm forever; His intentions can never be shaken" (Psalm 33:11 NLT).

Angela's Story

For as long as I can remember, I wanted to escape from my life—even at the tender age of five. After being molested at age six, I wanted to escape even more. I guess the pain became too much for me to bear, and when I was eleven I made my first mixed drink from my parents' liquor cabinet. I was home alone, and that buzz was the greatest feeling I had felt up to that time. I had kept the sexual abuse a secret for all those years, and thoughts of it being my fault tormented me every day, especially as I was going to sleep. I finally told my mom and thought that would help, but it didn't.

I don't blame all my feelings and actions on the abuse because I was depressed even before that. The death of my only surviving grandmother was the beginning of my addiction with cigarettes. I was a regular smoker by age fourteen. When the alcohol was no longer enough of an escape for me, I began using marijuana and LSD on a regular basis. I was a full-blown IV drug user and crack addict by age eighteen.

I also became very promiscuous, thinking I wasn't worth anything if the guy I was pursuing didn't accept my invitation for sex. My self-worth was determined by what guys thought of me. I never knew my true value because I never had a relationship with God. In fact, I thought He was punishing me, and I was angry with Him because I blamed Him for causing me so much pain. Before long, I decided there was no God, and there was no heaven or hell.

I was a totally different person when I was using. I was completely self-absorbed and always in search of my next fix, chasing that first rush. I totally disregarded anyone else's feelings. I would lie to my parents and brother all the time to get money or cover up my bruises and track marks from the drugs I was using intravenously. I only had one true friend, who is still by my side today, and I did not deserve her faithful friendship at all.

I began to steal from my parents to feed my addiction, and even did an illegal check scam to get a little bit of money to feed my lifestyle. Deep down I knew that was not the real me. I think my family and one true friend did, too, and that is why they stuck by me.

After almost fourteen years of addiction, I found myself at the lowest point in my life. I was living in one of the worst ghettos in town, and I was doing anything to survive and stay high, including prostitution. I was not eating, I was in an abusive relationship, and I was wasting away inside and out. I was being told I was evil and ugly, and I just wanted to die. So one day I tried to die by taking seventy of my prescription mood stabilizers. This put me into a coma for three days.

When I awoke, the first coherent words I heard came from the Lord. He said, "I have plans to prosper you." By the way, I had never read the Bible at that point in my life. An extended family member printed the Mercy Ministries application for me, and I knew that was my last option. I filled out that application all in one day while I was still in the hospital.

When I was at Mercy, being sober and not smoking brought to my attention other addictions, including food and sleep. It may sound silly, but working through my issues made me not want to feel, so I slept all the time. I think sleeping all the time delayed my healing process greatly, but I got it eventually. I truly believe I was miraculously healed from my addictions a few days after leaving the hospital, so I never had any cravings or temptations.

I was a little worried when I graduated Mercy, but I prayed all the time and kept reading my Bible every day. I was never really tempted with drugs or alcohol . . . I believe I was completely delivered from those desires. I do not even consider myself to still be an addict. I am a new creation in Christ Jesus!

Now, I just have good clean fun, and I don't hang out in bars or with those who may bring me down. When I first graduated from Mercy, I still felt a bit weak, but I chose to surround myself with strong Christians who I could learn from, and I continue to grow.

Honestly, I had a lot of fears after Mercy. Being a new Christian and living a completely different life was scary to me. 2 Timothy 1:7 was a verse I spoke out constantly. It brought me a lot of security to know God has not given me a spirit of fear, but of power, love, and a sound mind. Although I had betrayed Him and even rejected Him completely, He still loved me and comforted me.

While at Mercy, we would sing a worship song that says, "He lifted me from the miry clay and set my feet upon a rock." The scripture from which that line was taken, Psalm 40:2, became important to me, and there were times when I needed to remind myself what it says. Whenever I was going through a rough time, I would also remember Psalm 30:5: "Weeping may remain for a night, but rejoicing comes in the morning." Praise God that His mercies are new every morning. I am truly grateful for God's healing touch and that I am not who I used to be.

Monica's Story

The very first time I used drugs, I was thirteen. I was in eighth grade and had just moved back to the United States from Polynesia. This was a very hard time for me socially, and I honestly believed that by doing drugs, I would fit in. This proved to backfire, as I was ultimately labeled a "bad girl." I hated myself.

All through high school, I struggled with anger and an inability to deal with my emotions in a healthy manner. Neither of my parents were involved in my life, as they were too busy dealing with their own issues. Although I managed to do well in school and gain friends and popularity along the way, I still hated myself.

When I was seventeen, my father committed suicide after years of struggling with addiction. After his death, I rapidly headed down a path of destruction. I never doubted God was real, but ultimately, I felt insignificant to Him.

My drug addiction completely owned me. I rarely worked and couldn't keep my word for anything. I always had good intentions, but the drugs just overpowered my ability to operate in a healthy and reliable manner. I lost friends, jobs, and pretty much anything of any value in my life.

Cocaine is a powerful drug, and if used for prolonged amounts of time, cocaine-induced psychosis will occur. Essentially, you lose your mind and the ability to differentiate between what is real and what is not. Paranoia and irrationality become sources of comfort on some level because if you can feel them, at least you know you're alive. I turned into a crazy person—it's embarrassing to recall.

I finally hit rock bottom after about seven years of hard-core drug use. I remember lying on the floor in a state of panic. I had been up for days. I finally gave up. I couldn't do it anymore. I prayed for death, and I welcomed it. But in that moment I cried out, "God, if you're real, if you care, you have to do this for me because I just can't."

Three months later, I was a resident of Mercy Ministries in the Nashville home. (Thank you, Jesus!) During the Mercy application process, I learned that I was pregnant. This was an additional shock, but I do believe it was a huge part of what saved me. I now had something other than myself to live for.

My time at Mercy was definitely a time of healing. When I first arrived I was very angry, but God is so good. It's as though my transition from anger to peace was seamless. I remember the pain of facing things and how hard it was, but God was gentle with me. I don't think I've ever been more at peace with myself than when I lived in that home with forty other girls. (Imagine that!)

After I graduated following the birth of my son, I was blessed with an easy transition. I had a new baby, and the only thing I really had time for was him. The temptation to use was no longer lingering—I truly was a changed person! You don't have to cope; you can really become a new person through Christ and experience freedom from addiction.

Chapter Five

FOR PARENTS AND OTHERS WHO CARE

*A*ll kinds of addictions are prevalent in our society today, and obviously, families are greatly affected as a result. As a parent, you may be asking yourself many questions: Why is my daughter addicted? What do I do to help my daughter? What can I do to help myself deal with my daughter's addiction? This chapter will provide answers to those and other questions, as well as encourage you to persevere in your efforts to help your daughter.

Create an Environment that Cultivates Honesty

First of all, it is important to create an environment or atmosphere where your daughter can open up about her addiction. This will assist you in identifying the kind of help she needs. When consumed by an addiction, your daughter or loved one will most likely have tendencies to lie or manipulate. If your relationship with your daughter allows her to be honest, this will break down a lot of the barriers so you know how to help her.

Creating an environment that encourages genuine openness also means that you have to be willing to speak up when you sense manipulation taking place. There is a fine line between loving your daughter in a way that frees her to be transparent and enabling negative behavior to continue.

Confront in a Supportive Manner

Supportively confronting your daughter about her addiction is needed and cannot be avoided. If you avoid confronting your daughter and expect the issue to magically disappear, you will find yourself gravely disappointed. The best way to help your daughter is to confront her through the wisdom and guidance of the Holy Spirit. Before even speaking with your daughter, it would be wise to have a time of prayer asking God to help you as you help your daughter. Preparation in prayer is the best way to begin communication with your daughter. As you seek God for wisdom in confronting addiction, He will hear you and intervene.

Prayer for Your Daughter or Loved One

Lord God, I seek you in this time to give me wisdom in helping my daughter [or loved one]. I will be talking with her shortly to confront her about her addiction, and I need your guidance. I pray that I will speak your words and that those words will be anointed to break the bondage of addiction. I pray for my daughter's heart to be softened to hear you speak to her and that she will allow healing to begin in her life. I release freedom, healing, and love to flow in my daughter's life as well as my own. I thank you, God, for giving me strength in my daughter's journey to healing and wholeness. I submit this situation fully to you. In Jesus' name, Amen.

Before talking with your daughter, be sure to set up parameters to ensure an environment of honesty and safety. For example, choose a time when her friends and siblings are not present.

Depending on the situation, it may be necessary to have someone else with you, either your spouse or a trusted Christian friend.

Below is one example of a way to confront, get to the issue at hand, and offer help.

> Susan, I love you, and I always will. My love for you will never change regardless of what you have done in the past or what you will do in the future. Love involves me doing what is best for you, not just what you want. With that said, I need to ask you some questions, and I expect you to be honest with me. I will love you no matter what you say or what you will do, but I need you to be honest. What is going on right now? Are you using drugs again? I will do what I can to help you, but I need you to be willing to take the steps to receive help.

Create an Environment of Safety and Accountability

Creating an environment that offers safety and accountability will ensure that your daughter understands clear expectations within the family. Many times, the deception of addiction can cause those dealing with addictions to be secretive, rebellious, manipulative, and dishonest in order to avoid getting caught.

Parameters and boundaries are crucial to empower your daughter to see her choices clearly as well as the consequences for her choices. Parents must proactively work together to come up with a plan of action. (If you're a single parent, don't hesitate to ask for help from a trusted Christian friend, counselor, or pastor. You need support too!)

Those dealing with addiction often steal things to sell for drugs or other things they might need. You will need to create accountability and structure, and insist your daughter abide by the plan or face the consequences, including looking into other options for housing. It may be necessary to seek the help of an outside organization such as Mercy Ministries.

Face Addictions in the Family

Addiction can be a generational pattern that shows itself from grandmother to mother to daughter, for example, and often intensifies with each successive generation. When a generational pattern of addiction exists, only the power of God can break that stronghold and free the family.

Although God's power is greater than any addiction, the cooperation of family members will enhance and speed up your daughter's healing process. To help your daughter break free from addiction, the family needs to abstain from whatever substance your daughter is addicted to. They also need to provide a supportive atmosphere that empowers your daughter to walk out her freedom. If parents and/or other family members have addiction issues, your daughter may have difficulty breaking the addiction. Your daughter is responsible for her own actions, but the actions of family members can have a huge impact on your daughter—either making her journey tougher or easier. Encourage family members, as well as others in the community, to be respectful and choose behaviors that will encourage freedom for your daughter. In fact, it is hypocritical for you to ask your child or loved one to deal with her issues if you are not willing to deal with yours.

Prayer for a Parent Breaking Generational Patterns

Lord God, through the power of my God-given choice, I choose to live for you. I thank you that Galatians 3:13 says that in Christ the curse is broken. Through the power of the blood of Jesus shed at the cross and through the authority I have been given in Jesus' name, I break the power of addiction in my life, my family's life, and in the lives of my children. I choose life, and I thank you that this generational curse is broken, and a generation of blessing begins now. In Jesus' name, Amen.

Find Support

Parents need support when any family member is dealing with addiction. It is vital to have people in your life that can come alongside you in this journey of healing. Your support person (or team) may be a family member, pastor, counselor, friend, or mentor. Regardless of who you choose, the person should be someone you can trust and who will:

- Encourage Christian values
- Offer wisdom
- Live in the truth of God's Word
- Pray for you, your daughter, and other family members

Most of all, know that God will uphold you and strengthen you as you seek Him. He is your source and will be the biggest support for you and your daughter through the healing process.

CHANGING UNGODLY BELIEFS TO GODLY BELIEFS

Ungodly belief: I am alone, and no one cares how I feel or what I do.

Godly belief: God is always with me. He sees how I feel, and He comforts me.

Related Scriptures: "Cast all your anxiety on him because he cares for you" (1 Peter 5:7).

"The LORD himself goes before you and will be with you; he will never leave you nor forsake you. Do not be afraid; do not be discouraged" (Deuteronomy 31:8).

Ungodly Belief: I am too far gone to ever have hope of being free.

Godly Belief: God loves me with an everlasting love. Anything is possible with God because He is mighty to save.

Related Scriptures: "The LORD your God is with you, he is mighty to save. He will take great delight in you, he will quiet you with his love, he will rejoice over you with singing" (Zephaniah 3:17).

"The LORD appeared to us in the past, saying: 'I have loved you with an everlasting love; I have drawn you with loving-kindness'" (Jeremiah 31:3).

Ungodly Belief: The person I am on drugs is better than who I really am. No one would ever accept me for just me.

Godly Belief: God created me in His image, and I am accepted by Him.

Related Scriptures: "God created man in his own image, in the image of God he created him; male and female he created them" (Genesis 1:27).

"Accept one another, then, just as Christ accepted you, in order to bring praise to God" (Romans 15:7).

Ungodly Belief: I am worthless. I have no value and deserve nothing good.

Godly Belief: I have been blessed with every spiritual blessing. Because I am a child of God, I have an eternal inheritance in Heaven.

Related Scriptures: "Now we live with great expectation, and we have a priceless inheritance—an inheritance that is kept in heaven for you, pure and undefiled, beyond the reach of change and decay" (1 Peter 1:3–4 NLT).

"All praise to God, the Father of our Lord Jesus Christ, who has blessed us with every spiritual blessing in the heavenly realms because we are united with Christ" (Ephesians 1:3 NLT).

Ungodly Belief: I need a mind-altering substance because my mind is not good enough.

Godly Belief: I have the mind of Christ, and He gives me wisdom and knowledge through His Spirit.

Related Scriptures: "'For who has known the mind of the Lord that he may instruct him?' But we have the mind of Christ" (1 Corinthians 2:16).

"For the LORD gives wisdom, and from his mouth come knowledge and understanding" (Proverbs 2:6).

Ungodly Belief: I am emotionally unstable. I can stabilize my emotions when I am always high.

Godly Belief: The Holy Spirit lives inside of me—therefore, I have the fruit of the Spirit: love, joy, peace, patience, kindness, goodness, gentleness, faithfulness and self-control.

Related Scriptures: "The fruit of the Spirit is love, joy, peace, patience, kindness, goodness, gentleness, faithfulness and self-control" (Galatians 5:22–23).

"Hope does not disappoint us, because God has poured out his love into our hearts by the Holy Spirit, whom he has given us" (Romans 5:5).

Ungodly Belief: I have no control in my life, and the only time I am in control is when I use.

Godly Belief: God is in control of my life, and I can rest knowing that He directs my path and His plans are to prosper me and give me hope.

Related Scriptures: "'For I know the plans I have for you,' declares the LORD, 'plans to prosper you and not to harm you, plans to give you hope and a future'" (Jeremiah 29:11).

"He restores my soul. He guides me in paths of righteousness for his name's sake" (Psalm 23:3).

Ungodly Belief: I am a boring person and can only contribute fun and excitement through drugs and alcohol.

Godly Belief: I have a joy from the Lord that is better than any high. He brings life to my soul.

Related Scriptures: "The precepts of the LORD are right, giving joy to the heart. The commands of the LORD are radiant, giving light to the eyes" (Psalm 19:8).

"The LORD is my strength and my shield; my heart trusts in him, and I am helped. My heart leaps for joy and I will give thanks to him in song" (Psalm 28:7).

Ungodly Belief: I have no purpose and have nothing to live for beyond my next high.

Godly Belief: God has a purpose and a destiny for my life that is fulfilling and meaningful. He created me with an incredible eternal destiny for my life.

Related Scriptures: "No eye has seen, no ear has heard, no mind has conceived what God has prepared for those who love him" (1 Corinthians 2:9).

"Ask me and I will tell you remarkable secrets you do not know about things to come" (Jeremiah 33:3 NLT).

Ungodly Belief: It does not matter what I put in or do to my body, it is damaged and ugly anyway.

Godly Belief: My body is the temple of the Holy Spirit, and I will honor my body by taking care of it. By grace, God will restore me to wholeness, and I trust Him to heal any physical problems in His perfect timing.

Related Scriptures: "Do you not know that your body is a temple of the Holy Spirit, who is in you, whom you have received from God? You are not your own; you were bought at a price. Therefore honor God with your body" (1 Corinthians 6:19–20).

"I will restore them because I have compassion on them. They will be as though I had not rejected them, for I am the LORD their God and I will answer them" (Zechariah 10:6).

Ungodly Belief: Because I have lived a lie, I am unable to speak truth.

Godly Belief: I can speak truth because I am led by the Spirit of God. There is freedom in living an honest life.

Related Scriptures: "When the Spirit of truth comes, he will guide you into all truth. He will not speak on his own but will tell you what he has heard. He will tell you about the future" (John 16:13).

"Then you will know the truth, and the truth will set you free" (John 8:32).

Ungodly Belief: God could never forgive me after the horrible things that I have done and wrong choices that I have made.

Godly Belief: God delights to show grace. His forgiveness is endless, and His mercies are new every morning.

Related Scriptures: "Who is a God like you, who pardons sin and forgives the transgression of the remnant of his inheritance? You do not stay angry forever but delight to show mercy" (Micah 7:18).

"If we confess our sins, he is faithful and just and will forgive us our sins and purify us from all unrighteousness" (1 John 1:9).

INDEX TO PRAYERS

SOURCES

Alcorn, Nancy. *Keys to Walking in Freedom* CD series. Nashville: Mercy Ministries. (www.mercyministries.com).

Anderson, Neil T. *The Bondage Breaker.* Eugene, OR: Harvest House, 2006.

Anderson, Neil T. *Victory over the Darkness.* Ventura, CA: Regal, 2000. (www.ficm.org).

Capps, Charles. *God's Creative Power for Healing.* Tulsa: Harrison House, 1991. (www.charlescapps.com).

Kylstra, Chester, and Betsy Kylstra. *Restoring the Foundations.* Hendersonville, NC: Proclaiming His Word, Inc., 2001. (www.phw.org).

ABOUT MERCY MINISTRIES

*M*ercy Ministries exists to provide opportunities for young women to experience God's unconditional love, forgiveness, and life-transforming power. We provide residential programs free of charge to young women ages 13–28 who are dealing with life-controlling issues such as eating disorders, self-harm, addictions, sexual abuse, unplanned pregnancy, and depression. Our approach addresses the underlying roots of these issues by addressing the whole person—spiritual, physical, and emotional—and produces more than just changed behavior; the Mercy Ministries program changes hearts and stops destructive cycles.

Founded in 1983 by Nancy Alcorn, Mercy Ministries currently operates in three states and in Australia, Canada, New Zealand, Peru, and the UK, with plans for additional US and international locations underway. We are blessed to have connecting relationships with many different Christian congregations but are not affiliated with any church, organization, or denomination.

Residents enter Mercy Ministries on a voluntary basis and stay an average of six months. Our program includes life-skills training and educational opportunities that help ensure the success of our graduates. Our goal is for each young woman to not only complete the program but also to discover the purpose for her life and bring value to her community as a productive citizen.

For more information, visit our Web site at
www.mercyministries.com.

Mercy Ministries of America

www.mercyministries.com

Mercy Ministries Australia

www.mercyministries.com.au

Mercy Ministries Canada

www.mercycanada.com

Mercy Ministries UK

www.mercyministries.co.uk

Mercy Ministries New Zealand

www.mercyministries.org.nz

Mercy Ministries Peru

ABOUT THE AUTHOR

*D*uring and after college, Nancy Alcorn, a native Tennessean, spent eight years working for the state of Tennessee at a correctional facility for juvenile delinquent girls and investigating child abuse cases. Working for the state allowed her to experience firsthand the secular programs, which were not producing permanent results exemplified by changed lives. Nancy saw many of the girls pass the age of eighteen and end up in the women's prison system because they never got the real help they needed. She knew lasting change would never come as the result of any government system.

After working for the state, she was appointed Director of Women for Nashville Teen Challenge, where she worked for two years. Through her experience, she came to realize that only Jesus could bring restoration into the lives of these girls who were deeply hurting and desperately searching for something to fill the void they felt in their hearts. She knew God was revealing a destiny that would result in her stepping out to do something to help young women.

In January 1983, determined to establish a program in which lives would truly be transformed, Nancy moved to Monroe, Louisiana, to start Mercy Ministries of America. God instructed Nancy to do three specific things to ensure His blessings on the ministry: (1) not to take any state or federal funding that might limit the freedom to teach Christian principles, (2) to accept girls free of charge, and (3) to always give at least 10 percent of all Mercy Ministries' donations to other Christian organizations and ministries. As Nancy has continued to be faithful to these three principles, God has been faithful to provide for every need of the ministry just as He promised.

In Monroe, Nancy began with a small facility for troubled girls. After adding on twice to make additional space in the original home, Nancy began to see the need for an additional home to meet the special needs of unwed mothers. For this dream to be realized on a debt-free basis, Nancy knew she would need to raise funds. No doubt, God knew the need and already had a plan in place.

One day, Nancy, exhausted from speaking at an evangelism conference in Las Vegas, boarded a plane for home. The man sitting next to her seemed ready for a chat. When he asked her how much money she had lost gambling, Nancy told him she hadn't gone to Vegas to gamble and shared briefly about Mercy Ministries with him. He seemed interested, so Nancy gave him a brochure as they parted. About four weeks later, this same man called Nancy to ask her for more details about Mercy Ministries and said he felt compelled to help in some way. It was then that Nancy told him about the plans for the unwed mothers' home. He told her he had been adopted when he was five days old. His heart was so touched that he wrote a check to Mercy Ministries for the exact amount needed to help build the second Mercy Ministries house debt-free.

You can read Nancy's entire story in her book *Echoes of Mercy.*

To order additional copies of this title call:
1-877-421-READ (7323)
or please visit our Web site at
www.winepressbooks.com

If you enjoyed this quality custom-published book,
drop by our Web site for more books and information.

www.winepressgroup.com
"Your partner in custom publishing."

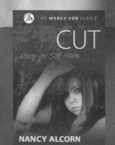